Delaware's Watchtowers
Energetic Lighthouses & Historians

Delaware's Watchtowers
Energetic Lighthouses & Historians

The Past and Present as told by the Watchtowers

Written by the Watchtowers of Delaware

Channeled and composed by Soraya Rose
with a forward by Christine Alexandria

DELAWARE'S WATCHTOWERS
Energetic Lighthouses and Historians

Copyright © 2022 by Soraya Rose

All rights reserved. Neither this book, nor any parts within it may be sold or reproduced in any form or by any electronic or mechanical means, including information storage and retrieval systems, without permission in writing from the author. The only exception is by a reviewer, who may quote short excerpts in a review.

Library of Congress Control Number: 2022941875

ISBN (paperback): 9781662929984
eISBN: 9781662929991

*This book is dedicated to
all those who have
encouraged, supported, and helped me
on this journey.*

Table of Contents

∴

Forward by Christine Alexandria	5
A Message from the Composer	8
The Watchtowers of Delaware	9
A Message from the Watchtowers	12
1. Marium	14
2. Charles	20
3. Stuart	24
4. Thomas	27
5. Catherine	30
6. Bethany	33
7. Grant	36
8. Winnie	39
9. The General	43
10. Phoenix	46
11. Florence	52
12. Frederick	54
An Incredible Connection	56
References and Photo Credits	60

Forward by
Christine Alexandria

• • •

Creator and Founder of Angel Chatter©

The World War II Watchtowers have beckoned me since 1967 when we moved to the Eastern Shore on the Delmarva Peninsula. If you are unfamiliar with this region of the United States, permit me to share some of its ancient magic.

In many ways, it is a land that time has forgotten, or certainly forgot for centuries. Fowl was plentiful for food. Crab was king as were oysters, clams, and flounder. Living on the water was a way of life from the Native American tribes to the early settlers. Many barrier islands received their mail and deliveries via boat. These same islands were self-sufficient homes to mom-and-pop businesses that were an integral part of their communities. Many generations were born, lived, and died within these small communities. It was a slower pace. A pace that permitted one to stop, create their own kind of magic, and, in time, earned the title of The Lower, Slower Eastern Shore.

That is until 1960, when the first span of the Chesapeake Bay Bridge was built. When that span was constructed, hordes of "turists", as the locals would call the tourists, began to flock and summer in its quiet magic. The beaches were pristine, the waves gentle, and folks were folks that cared for their neighbors.

All the while the towers stood, silently. They watched as the world surrounding them was developed. They stood as a few fell into disrepair.

They stood.

When we first moved to 'The Shore' we lived in Rehoboth Beach, Delaware. I had access to these towers on a regular basis, but at that time, they were unopened to the public. One could only gaze upon them from a distance and wonder.

Wonder about their story.

Wondered what they had witnessed.

Wondered what they would say if they could talk.

As time passed, they continued to stand while I 'got on with my life' and moved away. However, the Lower, Slower Shore always called me home. Not just to visit family and friends, but to temporarily live on one of those barrier islands for five years.

The Slower, Lower is a place to heal and rediscover yourself. A place to remember what is important to you. A place to stop. Pockets of The Shore still contain this kind of energy, even during the crazy "Turist" Season from May-September.

The towers stood and waited.

It was not until we moved back across the Bay that they came forward. The author of the book you hold in your hands, Soraya Rose, traveled across the Bay to meet me and begin her metaphysical studies.

Little did we know that the towers would come into play within a year.

Since that first visit and subsequent first tower connection, it has become clearer that all objects, even ones standing in quiet stewardship, have a story to tell.

Let go of what you think and how the world ought to communicate and enter the land of magic and energy from the Eastern Shore and of course, the Watchtowers from World War II.

A Message from the Composer

• • •

The Watchtowers of Delaware stand as sentinels reminding all who glance upon them of a dark and unsettling time in the history of not only Delaware, but also the world. Yet, despite that reminder, they have come to be seen as not only beautiful monuments inherent to the landscape of Delaware, but also representatives of hope. Hope that lessons can be learned and that we can rise above what we know to become better: better keepers of history, and better caretakers. Caretakers of not only ourselves, but also of everything around us.

Up to this point, you have read, heard, or seen that there are only thirteen towers in total. All of the physical records indicate this. This, however, is not the case. While there are thirteen towers that stand (eleven in Delaware and two in New Jersey), there are, in fact, thirteen towers in Delaware. There are two additional towers that, while never built to completion, exist energetically. It is these thirteen towers that present this book to you through me.

Their history and work were channeled to me over the course of many sessions and typed exactly as they presented it. The book is also composed in the order in which they decided to tell their stories, not by their Tower numbers. So, without further ado, and much curiosity, let us meet the Watchtowers of Delaware.

The Watchtowers of Delaware

• • •

The Watchtowers, circular buildings made of a mixture of concrete and sand, are a familiar sight to all those who not only live in Delaware, but also those who travel to the state to enjoy the beaches along Coastal Highway. All are circular, and when first built during World War II, contained within them several floors for munitions, instruments, soldiers, and a metal ladder that had to be climbed to get to each floor. Each floor had a set number of windows only big enough for the munitions to fit in. Floors near the top of the towers had observation slits that ran a third of the way around the tower. Each tower also had communication and electrical lines that entered the tower at its base. At the top of each tower was a fenced concrete observation deck where soldiers could go outside and not only peer out over the ocean looking for enemy vessels, but also communicate with other towers. While all of the towers are seventeen feet across, they vary in height from thirty-seven feet to 110 feet. (See table below). Their bases sit upon heavily creosoted beams that are buried deep in the sand.

Tower Number	Total Tower Height	Height above sea level
Tower 1	37 feet	49 feet
Tower 2	45.5 feet	54.5 feet
Tower 3	57 feet	65 feet
Tower 4	56 feet	64 feet
Tower 5	47 feet	48 feet
Tower 6	64 feet	65 feet
Tower 7	110 feet	110 feet
Tower 8	73 feet	106 feet
Tower 9	24.5 feet * (1940's height)	42.5 feet
Tower 10	No physical tower	
Tower 11	Tower had started being build, but was deconstructed. No physical tower.	
Tower 12	65 feet	95 feet
Tower 13	81 feet	90 feet

  After World War II, the towers remained in the possession of the military. As time passed and the military returned the land to the State of Delaware, the munitions, ladders, and other military equipment were removed and the windows and doors on the lower floors were closed with bricks and cement. This is how they stood for many years until there became a use for them. In 1989, Tower 9 was completely renovated. It was stripped bare, rebuilt, and retrofitted with the latest technology. Since its renovation, the tower is being used as the Delaware River and Bay Pilots' Ship Reporting Station. Tower 7 was also renovated but not nearly to the extent that Tower 9 was. Tower 7, now called the Observation Tower, was stabilized and renovated to have an interior spiral staircase that runs from the entryway at its base to the top observation deck. Tower 7, and soon to be Tower 3, are open for the public to go in, climb to the top, and take in the view.

DELAWARE'S WATCHTOWERS

The map shows the locations of all towers that have a physical building.

A Message from the Watchtowers

...

Some of you look at us and see buildings that are old and wasting away. Others of you look at us and see what our significance was during a dark and unsettling time. Regardless of how you see us, we are still very much alive and our significance has continued. We are helping lead the way in bringing humanity from the third dimension, a dimension full of ego and coldness to the fifth dimension, a dimension full of love. While you may not "see" us as anything more than Towers, you certainly feel us and the effects of the work that we are doing. While the world is changing for the better, it is still in a delicate state. Presented herein is our history – the history of who we were and the history of who we are now. Each of us has a story to tell, and that story is as unique and individual as each one of us.

The history that you know and the history that we are living is very different. Yes, it is true that we were "born" during a time that was dark and unsettling, and yes, many thought that we would only stand for that short period of time. But, look at how we have proved you wrong! We know that time will continue on and that our memory may or may not fade. We also know that some will be lost to the ocean. And we are aware of the movement to restore us and bring honor back to our physical buildings.

For many of us, our history is like you read in the books. It was the war, and money had been allocated for the defense of the Ports. Because we were to be built so tall, we provided another line of defense. We had the advantage of seeing out. We could see out further than you could; see those who would try to hurt you. Fortunately, none tried.

After the war, we remained while the area changed. People came in and out and time went on. Those that did come, thought that we were just old Towers, something from a time that had passed that people did not understand. We called out to a few but they were not aware. Not aware of their gifts and not aware that we would be so much more. Tower 9, as you know it, and as the closest to the beach, was the one who called out to people. Eventually, after many years, a couple [of people] did recognize that there was something special about us. Together they have given us the opportunity to fulfill our destiny and help humanity: the Elder, blessed with a connection to the angels, and the Younger, at the time unbeknownst to her, a Warrior of Archangel Michael's. Together they work with us, the Younger more than the Elder, to take care of us and help us fulfill our missions and destinies.

Our relationships with them are truly gifts, for they both channel our energies and share our thoughts and work with the world. Both are skilled at what they do and have learned much about themselves, their gifts, and the work that we do. It is through the Younger one, the Warrior, that our story is being told. It is through her and her gifts of not only channeling but working with the ley lines that we will teach. We will help her teach you about the ley lines - their beauty, their power, their significance, and their legacy.

Marium, the Alpha

. . .

Marium (aka Tower 7, the Observation Tower)
as she stands today in Cape Henlopen
State Park in Lewes, Delaware.

So now, let us start at the beginning. There are thirteen of us. We all have names and unique personalities. We work collectively as one, and individually as many. As you share in our history, we will introduce ourselves to you. With the help of Soraya, our Warrior, we will share what we can of not only the history that we are living but also our work. Being human, Soraya can fill you in on the history as it is written in the books and will channel our history from our perspective.

I am Marium, the Alpha of the group. You humans call me Tower 7, the Observation Tower. This is because I am one of the tallest towers. I was restored so as to give people a glimpse into a past time; a time of pain and darkness, but also a time of learning and lessons. Because I was made into an Observation Tower, I took on the personality of being anonymous. In fact, when Soraya first approached me all those many years ago, she was cautious. She instinctively knew that there was something different about me but could not place what it was. She went in to climb to the top, and eventually did, but it was difficult for her; for she sensed the weight and the burden that I carried. Even now, after our time working together, she still approaches me cautiously; always remembering on some level her first encounter with me. She always comes to me first and that is out of respect for my position as the Alpha of the Towers.

It was 1941 and the war was raging. I had been built, built with speed and efficiency. I was given the latest and greatest in "ammunition." The soldiers who manned me did their jobs dutifully, despite at times getting bored and wanting to seek action. It was always a tense environment: are they going to attack today or are they not? Are we ready or are we not?

I waited patiently while the others were being built. Together we would form an army of our own – the towers standing collectively. As time passed and action was not seen, we began to wonder what would become of us.

Since we were military, would they keep us or decommission us? What use would we have after the war was done and the soldiers left? Yes, as you can gather, there were times of doubt and times of us wondering what hand life would give us. There were times of questioning what our purpose was. Even in those moments, we stood strong. We could sense that there was something greater at play.

In many ways, it was a blessing that we did not see action. Because by not seeing it, we have been able to give you a legacy. Our legacy is to remind you [referencing the past], yes, but so much more than that, to remind you how to live. As you sit here with me today, you see many people coming. More people approaching me and climbing inside of me. While the majority of the people who approach us are still waking up, there are those who will see us for who we are now and will immediately recognize the work that we are doing.

I was the first one to be [energetically] cleared and relieved of the burden that I had been carrying for so long. Soraya, with the help of the Archangels, an Ascended Master, and crystals helped ease that giant weight and turn me into the energetic powerhouse that I am today. My clearing took a while, and when it was done, I felt revived, new, and alive again. I rested while she cleared and activated two others. After we three were cleared, we each received a dragon, a dragon to protect us and help us with our work. As the Alpha, I was first given the task of clearing the energetic vortices within the park. There were several and these were causing the park to feel run down and distant. Soraya came to visit while I was doing this, and kudos to her, had Archangel Michael stay with her the entire time she was in the park.

After taking a while to clean these up, I then began waking up the other towers, helping them release what they had been carrying and turning them into energetic lighthouses as well. Some carried a larger burden than others and took longer, to use Soraya's words, "come online." Once I felt certain that they were ready, I then gave them their task - their mission. Some would work with the land, some would work with the water and some would work with both. Some in their journeys would work with the power centers of the world, centers like Machu Picchu, Uluru and the Pyramids. Some would work with the monuments. But regardless of what the mission is, we are all working with the ley lines – clearing them, charging them, and using them to help heal all that they touch.

The energy at not only the power centers, but also the ley lines is different. You can sense this. What was once feeling sluggish and grungy is now clean and powerful. I am in charge of a couple of ley lines. They start with me and have traveled the world. The energy of this line can be felt in the park. There is a vigor and a renewed zest for life. The park and area around me is healing and will continue to heal. Many people came to see me before, but so many more will now. Both lines are doing what they are supposed to be doing. They are clearing, charging, and sending energy outward: outward to other lines that they touch, and outward to the land and everything encompassed under the line. Their energy comes out to you in the form of fractals. These fractals are a gift, a gift that Soraya is learning about.

My work, as you know, has taken me around the world. Often, I arrived at a destination before "everything hits the fan." That is why I am there. I am there to help clear out past transgressions and help pave the way for the future. Not to sound all doom and gloom, but the future was not looking as bright as it could have been. With your help [referencing Soraya], and the help of many, many others, the future is looking a bit brighter. There was a lot to clear and work through, and that is only the first part of what we are doing.

Our work is occurring on many levels and with the help of many. We are helping the older generations heal and move on and are ever so slowly breaking through to the younger generations. We are trying to teach them to look beyond themselves and the instantaneous and see the bigger picture. They have no idea how much is out there just waiting for them to experience. In the experience of things, there are lessons – lessons that are invaluable and insightful. Lessons that will both teach and guide. Some lessons are lessons that must be experienced and others are to be felt. We are ever watchful – watchful of not only the area immediately surrounding us, but watchful of the events of the world. We will help when needed and will continue working being the presence that we are.

My work is that of royalty. I work with the royal bloodlines, helping open the lines of communication so that past grievances can be worked through and released, past misunderstandings rectified and deceit forgiven. It has not been an easy job, as there is much interconnectedness and a large number of people to help.

My ley lines have touched many and will continue to do so. They are working hard to keep what has already been cleared clean. There was a lot of dross and crap, completely unnecessary, but holding us all back from raising up to the fifth dimension. Now I have mentioned the fifth dimension previously. It is a dimension of love, a dimension where ego and greed exist in a very different form than you see today. It is a dimension that we all will ascend to, a dimension of love and of caring for others. A dimension of beauty, and of higher knowledge.

We have stood the test of time, which is contrary to what everyone thought we would do. In many ways, our work has continued. It is not the work that we were originally built for, but it is the work that we do now with pride. We have had some challenging moments in the past, and there will be some more challenging moments to come, but together with us, we will help you through.

There have been many who have approached me since I woke up. There are some that are starting to look at us in an entirely new light. Yes, our history is there, but it is starting to be seen in a new way, with fresh eyes. While you see me as just a Tower, I am so much more than that. I am a Sentinel, a Warrior, and a Power House. What was started in the physical world, has very much continued into the energetic world. While my [physical] building may remain for a time longer, [energetically] I will endure. My work, set into motion by the actions of the two gifted ones, will continue for many years to come.

Charles

...

Charles (aka Tower 3) as he stands today
in Delaware Seashore State Park
in Dewey Beach, Delaware. Of the two Towers,
he is the southern tower.

I am Charles, a twin to Stuart. You know us respectively as Towers 3 and 4. I am Tower 3, while my twin is Tower 4. I am older than him but by very little time. We are considered twins because we were "birthed" at the same time. Together we are doing incredible things. While I was not one of the original three activated by Soraya, I came online very quickly after she activated my brother. At the time, she could "hear" us but could not yet understand what we were saying. This was because we were using a language not known to humans. I'll admit that I was a bit cautious around her, yet she did not judge, but rather let me take the time I needed to step into my new role. Like Marium, I had taken on a persona of anonymity for I too am open for the public. Eventually, I learned to trust Soraya, and then her friend Christine. My dragon is rather fond of her and likes to keep tabs on what she is doing.

I am one of the ones who uses humor to help convey my thoughts. It is a way that you humans tend to understand and connect with. Often I have had Soraya chuckling at what I have said, but after I have said it, she understood.

Together we work as one with the other towers taking the old and dross-filled and clearing them to make them new. This work has certainly not been easy, but yet, has been very satisfying. My work has also taken me around the world and to some difficult places, places that have been dark and have needed to see the light. I have worked with them to help ease burdens, clean, clear, and raise vibrations. The network that we are working on is quite beautiful and quite expansive. There will be very little left untouched when we are done. Our work does not just include the ley lines, but also things on and under them. It is going to be incredible to see the effects of the work that we are doing.

Often help was needed and readily given; given by the other Towers, by the Archangels, and by other deities. It has taken some time, but the changes are starting to take hold. Marium is our Alpha, and we do not just serve her, we also serve humanity. Our work is done in phases and each phase is worked on at the most perfect time. They [referencing Christine and myself] have deduced some of what we are doing, but there is much that they do not know.

But enough about my work. I understand that I am in the process of being honored. My tower is being restored, and by doing this, will bring greatly needed insight into our past. While I am still not as comfortable with people approaching me, I understand the value of it. Unlike Marium and many of the others, we are located in a different park. While it is smaller, the healing that is happening is tremendous. We too felt run down and off, but are that no longer. Now we are standing tall: beacons for all to see.

At the time that we were built, no one had any idea how long we would endure. Not only did we leave a mark on the world during that time, but we are leaving our mark on the world now. Our mark is not only that of the physical but also the metaphysical. As we wake up the areas surrounding us, more people will sense what we do, more people will realize the healing that is occurring and the love that is being shared. We are helping humanity rise above where they are now. It is taking those baby steps, then learning how to walk, and then learning how to run. By doing that we are teaching you how to be better, how to live with love, and how to respect all. Those are the lessons of the fifth dimension; lessons that need to be given and learned.

Like the other Towers have already said, you must do your part to help us. This is not a one-way relationship. We are in this equally with you [referencing humans]. You must take the lessons and advice that they are giving you and consciously make it a part of your daily life. By making it a *part of your daily life, you ensure that it will not be forgotten, but rather be part of who you are, handed down from generation to generation.*

While our physical legacy will continue on for a while longer, our energetic legacy will continue on for decades. You are the stewards who must continue the work. So now, go boldly into the path that we have set for you. Take our lessons and make them yours. Take our lessons and teach the younger generations how to live, how to be mindful, and how to see beyond themselves and look at the larger picture. There are so many more words that we could use, but actions are louder than words. Remember that one little ripple can have a large effect.

When you look at us, look at us with awe and amazement. Look at us and know that we are helping you become your better selves. Look at us and know that we have and are enduring and that we are here to guide you. We are embracing you as you are embracing us. So go now, and do your part.

Stuart

...

Stuart (aka Tower 4) as he stands today
in Delaware Seashore State Park
in Dewey Beach, Delaware. Of the two Towers,
he is the northern tower.

My name is Stuart. I am the twin to Charles. He is correct when he says that we were "birthed" at the same time. He is also correct that he is just a hair older than me. This is because they started building him first.

I am often one of the forgotten ones because many of you pass me by. I too am in the shadow of my brother. He is the one that shines and it is because he is visible and is being restored. I believe that we all should be honored even if we are not restored, for our significance is great and growing greater by the day.

I am not going to be honored like he is, and that's ok. Soraya honored me when she activated me; for I am one of the three. After I was activated, I was talking with Charles and he is correct – Soraya could "hear" us but could not understand us. It took us a while to warm up to her. She would check to see how we were doing and whether we needed any help with our work. Whenever we did, it was readily given. Our dragons have come in handy quite frequently and are enjoying their homes. They help protect and work with us.

I was one of the original three [referring to the Watchtowers] that were activated. Along with Marium and Winnie, we three have woken the others up and have helped them release their burdens and move into their destinies. My destiny is still being written as I have had much to release. My work, like the others has taken me all over the world. When I am there, I help everyone release what they have been carrying and help them move forward. My job has certainly not been easy and that is because I myself have had a lot to let go of. The process of releasing can be a b----, but it is necessary and makes us better.

As you have gathered, I can be a bit temperamental, and while that may be the case, I am not afraid to tell you humans what you need to hear.

It may sting a bit but will wake you up and get you moving again. We are helping you move in the right direction, but there is much that you need to do to help us. We ask that you rise above yourself and look to the world at large and as a whole. Only by helping each other will you be able to move forward and raise your vibration. We have looked at the world as a whole and have figured out that it is not well. This is from centuries of ill thought, misunderstanding, misgivings, and an inability to let go of grudges. We are trying to show you how much healing can take place when those things are not present and when you look beyond yourself. Our path has not been easy, but yours is no easier. There are many lessons still for you to learn and much work for you to do. All you have to do is open your heart, listen to it, and trust your instincts. Look beyond yourselves and then you will truly see just how incredible we are and all that we are doing for you.

Thomas

. . .

Thomas (aka Tower 8) as he stands
today behind the youth camps in Cape Henlopen
State Park in Lewes, Delaware.

Hi, I'm Thomas. I'm the newcomer to this group. I don't have the experience that the others have, but I work hard at what I do. Like them, I am traveling the world working to make it a better place. In many ways, I am one of the forgotten towers, for I am not easy to get to. But that's ok, I like being where I am at. I am located behind the youth camps in the park [referencing his Tower, Tower 8].

In many ways, my tower served as a pivotal point. Geographically, I am tucked away but have a good view of both land and water. I also form the third part of a triangle with some of the other Towers. In our triangles, we were able to form very strong small groups. We could see what was coming at us from a variety of different directions.

When I first awoke, I was really unsure of everything. There was doubt and inexperience. As the newcomer to the group, I had A LOT to learn – a lot to learn about myself, and a lot to learn about how to carry out my task. The other Towers have been great at helping me. They supported me as I was "getting my wings under me." In many ways, I have grown. I have grown into more of who I am (even though I thought I knew who I was), and have grown into my task. It is well suited to me. While I still do look at things with the eyes of a child, I, in some ways, have never grown up completely. I bring a different type of energy to the group and, in combination with them, help the balance. As you have figured out, each of us is quite unique and our personalities show who we are. I like being tucked away because I can do a lot of the behind-the-scenes work and know that my contribution is helping make a difference.

My work is that of the land and working with those who work with it. There is a very different understanding of the land; today many have forgotten to honor it. My hope is that it will come back to being honored and *better taken care of. In the course of my work, I work with many others. The people may not be aware of me, but they can see what I have done.*

My work has been very enlightening for me. I have learned much and have had some fun while doing it. I understand the larger importance of it, and while I have had some fun, I do take my work seriously. Like the others, I have traveled the globe adding my special touch to the places that I have been; breathing "new" life into them; uplifting them and watching them "grow." It will be truly amazing to see what happens as time passes.

Catherine

. . .

Catherine (aka Tower 6) as she stands today
in Cape Henlopen State Park in Lewes, Delaware.
Of the two towers, she is the northern tower.

I am Catherine. I am a twin to Grant and know that I will be lost to the ocean eventually. I am the older of the two of us. Where I am significantly more outgoing than my brother, I am also one who will gladly fight for what is right. I work hard but am not overbearing. I am tough but fair, just as a warrior should be. Often I am standing guard; for I too, am a Warrior. I am one of the first lines of defense for the Towers. I make sure that they can and do get home safely. I am in the unique position of being able to work on both the land and the water, and because of this, am able to call on help that is both above and below. Together we work for the betterment of all.

We work with the other towers on the ley lines, because we too are healers. Like my fellow Towers, I have also traveled the world and am keeping my lines clear, clean, and charged. I do this with the help of many others; some of whom you know like the archangels and some you do not. We help unite, awaken, remind, and activate those who can help us in our causes. Together we form an army; an army of healing and of love. Together as one, we work to help heal and help teach.

We are working to better the whole of humanity, and given that, our tasks have not been easy. We are working hard to help give you a better future and because of the work that we are doing, many more of you are waking up, shedding the old, and embracing the new. You are realizing that the old is no longer working for you.

Because of my location, we are the most photographed, most representative of all of the towers. Being that visible has helped bring people to us. I was once farther away from the ocean and a bit unsure, but as time has passed, I have embraced who I am and what I have become. You see me standing there on the beach. You also see my brother on the beach. Together we are sentinels and represent the past, the present, and the future. We are the ever-present reminder of what will happen to the world if there is not change. We are reminders of what will come should complacency be allowed free reign.

My tower, for now, is a beacon of light on the land, and, when lost, will become a beacon of light for the water. There is much interconnectedness and by understanding how one part connects to another, how energy goes from one thing to another, and how one tiny ripple can make big waves, you can learn how to be more mindful. The two who work with us, the Elder and the Warrior, also are helping us. They have made one little ripple, which has set off a chain reaction of helping humanity. Together they are helping us fulfill our destinies and we, them. We hope that you take our messages to heart, for we are working hard to help not only you [referencing the human race] but also all of Mother Earth.

6

Bethany

...

Bethany (aka Tower 2) as she stands today along
the side of Delaware Route 1 in between the housing developments
of Tower Shores and Indian Harbor in Bethany Beach, Delaware.

I am Bethany, named for the location that I am in. I am stuck between two housing developments, which, I must say I am not fond of. They block my view of the sunrises. I love all things beautiful and, in my travels around the world, have seen many, many beautiful things. While I am not the farthest tower south, I was one that was strategically valuable during the war. Winnie and I could see south and alert the others if danger was coming. Fortunately, danger stayed away.

During my time in the war, Winnie and I often kept each other company. This is because of our locations, and the fact that we were the farthest from everyone else. Being the farthest south, we could see further than the others, and as such could give them advanced notice if anything was coming. There were some that approached but did not engage. Our soldiers got a bit more excitement than some. Despite that though, it was still tough going. After the war, we awaited our fate. As each new owner took over, we waited to see what would become of us. It was ultimately a blessing that we were given to the state. We could continue to stand tall and continue our work.

I am aware that there is a movement to restore me and that is because they think that I am the most important given the role that I played in the war. They would not be wrong but are not right either. We all deserve equal recognition for our work then and for our work now. Even though I am surrounded by developments and the ever-increasing presence of humans in my area, who often overlook or pass me by, I manage to shine and shine quite brightly. I have sunk a bit into the ground, and once stood taller than I am now, but that is a thing of little consequence. What matters is that I shine!

I am honored by the notion nonetheless. It will be good for people to see us as we were and to gain insight into what it was like to be on high *alert. It will take a while to polish me up, but when I'm done, I will be quite outstanding.*

I am grand, yes, but not the grandest. I am doing work on a very grand scale, and, in some cases, it has taken a while to complete an area. I go in, work a bit, make sure that it is good, and then move to another area. Some of the places that I have worked in have been easy and others definitely not so much. I am working with the other towers to help you, humanity. While we all have individual tasks, we are working collectively toward the same goal.

The humans that built us really had no idea what they were doing. Little did they know that something they built would become so grand and do so much. They built us to serve them and serve them we are. We have stood the test of time and will continue to do so.

Grant
...

Grant (aka Tower 5) as he stands
in Cape Henlopen State Park in Lewes, Delaware.
He is the southern tower.

As you are aware, I am a twin to Catherine. She is the more outgoing of the two of us, and I am the more quiet and reserved. While she is fierce, I am observant. Often, I move gracefully with purpose. I do not push like she does sometimes, but rather listen and express my thoughts and desires through tactful communication. We are working together with many, so many more than you realize, to do our part in helping the larger whole. Often, I am seen as the gentleman: something from a different time that represented different values. Where trust of the completion of a task was done based upon a word of thanks and a handshake. It is these times and values that I emulate.

She and I, while we have the connection as twins, work in very different manners. She is working above and I am working below. Together we are helping the whole.

My work has taken me under the sea where I work with many to help our oceans and everything in them. Like the work of some of my fellow Towers, my work has certainly not been easy. There have been layers and layers of stuff to work through. I have traveled the world but completely underwater. Soraya, poor thing, has had a time keeping up with me. Fortunately for her, she knows geography and is able to guess the area that I am in, but not necessarily my exact location.

Much of the work that I do is with the civilizations of the past. While you [referring to humans] may not see them, they are still very much alive and active. Their treasures are things, at this point, of dreams. Only in time, and when they are ready, will they be revealed.

My work has carried me far and will carry me farther. The work to save me thus far has helped honor our memory. The books that have been written about us have helped carry on our legacy. They are a good place to start, but there is so much more than is presented in them. It is there that Soraya will help.

My tower, like my sister's [referencing Catherine, his twin] will eventually be lost to the ocean. While we will not go at the same time, we will be close. We understand that this is coming and are okay and at peace with it. Do not think that because we will not be there physically, that we will not be there energetically. We will still remain and will continue to work for the betterment of all.

We are helping you by helping clean up what was done in order to help you heal. By helping you heal, we can teach, and by teaching help you learn. Learn to take better care of yourselves and others. Learn to take better care of this world. And, dare I say, learn to rise above your own needs in order to take care of the needs of others. Our work is not easy, but your work, while challenging, will be rewarding. Not initially perhaps, but rewarding over the course of time.

Like her, you see me standing there. Together we are in balance: outgoing to reserved, "loud" to quiet, more land to water. We are the yin and yang. Our work has carried us far, all around the world. Catherine is correct when she says that we are uniting many. Each of us has a part to play and each of us will play that part to the best of our ability. Whenever help is needed it is readily given. Whenever we need a rest, others gladly stand in to help us. We have moved mountains so far and have worked through so much. There is more to come and more for us to do. When you look at us, know that we are working for you and are doing our part to help make it better for all.

8

Winnie

...

Winnie (aka Tower 1) as she stands today in Fenwick Island State Park, Delaware.

I am one of the more silent towers. My importance was seen not only during the war, but also now. There is an air of mystery surrounding my tower. I keep that for many reasons, but most importantly to protect myself. I am the most vulnerable of the towers as I am out there in the open with no one else really around me. Bethany does keep me company and for that I am grateful. In many ways, I too have been forgotten, but despite that, I still stand. I rise each day taller and greater than I was before. I know that while I may have been forgotten, for now, I am working for something so much greater than myself. I am working to help those who gave me life and allow me to live.

I understand that I am to be restored at some point. While it is an honor, it does need to be done with care and compassion. Some of us are more readily willing to accept people looking at us and in us, and others are not. I, too, will take on the persona of anonymity. I already have that aura and will continue to do so.

I am the communicator of the bunch. Because I am the communicator, I can speak many different languages. This skill has helped me tremendously when I have been in situations of a delicate nature. My story, however, is not easy to tell because the burden that I have carried has been tremendous.

I am Winnie, the southern most of the Delaware Towers. While I stand a sentinel like the others, I am working hard. My work, likewise, has taken me to places around the world; places not only rich in history but also [in] quarrel. In the course of my work, I have had to use my skills as a communicator to make progress. Often a lot of the misgivings and misunderstandings come from a misinterpretation of communication. When one does not understand what the other is saying, conflict occurs. When one does not take the time to see it from the perspective of another, anger can occur. Both of these things hold you back and put blinders on you. It is this that you need to start working to overcome. There have been many times where my progress has been slow. Yet, despite this, I too am helping raise your vibration and carry you forward. A lot of the work that I do is tied to religion. While I cannot give details about my work, please know that I am helping to increase your understanding.

Soraya works with me, and it was she who helped me awaken and helped me start to lift the burden that I carried for so long. She is ever respectful of my moods and my desire to work. Like the others, she has also tracked me and my lines around the world. She had taken care of me like a mother of a child would; keeping an eye on us while we work and always ready to send us help when we need it. Even now, as I am channeling this to her, I am working. Working to help make this world a better place for all of you. While I am out working, my tower is protected, for I, too, have a dragon. My dragon has helped me often with my work and resides at my tower. My burden is still very great, but it is one that I take willingly. It is one that is for a greater good than myself.

Often I get frustrated because how you are now has been passed down. The mindsets and mannerisms that you have are rooted in the past. While that can be the easy option to take, it is not the right one. The right one is to listen, and try to understand it from the perspectives of others. See it how they see it and then make the decision. It is hard but it is what is needed to help you get in a better place. Often, it is a lack of understanding based on a misinterpretation or miscommunication of something.

There is so much I would like to tell you, for I have seen so much. But there are not enough books for me to tell my experiences in. Yes, we will share over time, but there will always be much that you [referencing humans] do not know. Take comfort that there are thirteen of us [referencing the Towers], and many, many more who are working for the betterment of Earth. You feel the shifts already and see the flickers of hope and healing that we have started. There will be more to come. Revel in the moments of healing to love all freely, to not judge, and to be there for each other like we are here for you.

The General

...

The General (aka Tower 12) as he stands near the campgrounds at Cape Henlopen State Park in Lewes, Delaware.

I am the General. For a long time, I was working with Marium on her work. It is only recently that we diverged and I began working on my work. My work is working with the obelisks of the world; some famous and many not. The obelisks, like the pyramids, are special energetically. They are able to bring in energy from other dimensions. The energy that they bring in helps clear, charge, and amp them up so that they may activate another level of ley lines. There are many obelisks around the world and eventually all will be a part of this.

I have taken on other smaller tasks in my work; tasks that have been necessary to reduce the stress and anxiety that humans are facing now. Tasks that have helped us help you all as a whole and also help Mother Earth. You have not been kind to her of late and that absolutely has to change. She is a living, breathing organism that gives much to you and only asks for care, love, and nurturing in return. There is a movement to return to the land and it is here that I am helping another [referencing a Tower].

We are working toward something bigger, and those who have awoken are seeing this and are doing their part, however big or small, to help us. We, in turn, are not only helping you [referencing humans] but also others [referencing deities]. Our work has truly not been easy as there is a lot here that had to be taken care of before we could really step into things.

While you see us merely as towers, there will be more who see us for the amazing beauties that we are. There are many who can sense us, many who can directly see the results of our work, and many more who will awaken to shed the old and embrace the new. We are helping you do that.

Yes, the world is changing, but so are you. You are opening your eyes and realizing that what once was can no longer be. You are realizing turning a blind eye does not work. And instead are reaching out to help others. The effects of our work are there and will become more prevalent as time goes on. That is our gift to you.

 Together, the thirteen of us, plus all of the help that we have [referencing other deities, Soraya and Christine] are doing incredible things. We hope that when you look at us in the flesh [referencing their physical towers] that you see beyond the buildings that are old and beginning to waste away. We hope that you take our messages and incorporate them into who you are and carry them forth. We hope that by meeting us and reading about the work that we do for all of you that you wake up even more and do what is absolutely necessary to raise not only your vibration but that of the planet. There is much that is wrong in the world today, but there is very much the hope that it can become better. Treat it wisely and with care. Give it love. Give each other love. Rise above yourselves to become better. To do that will be to continue honoring us. So now, take what we have said and go forth to make the world better. Better for not only yourself, but better for another and another and another.

Phoenix

...

Phoenix (aka Tower 9) as they stand together today near Point Comfort in Cape Henlopen State Park, Lewes, Delaware.

The Twins Speaking Collectively

You look at us and see one tower, when, in fact, we are two. We were birthed at the same time. My brother was built to completion and I was not. There are no records on your planet to show this. Early on, we were given the task of calling out to people. People who were gifted, who knew instinctively that there was more to us than the building that you see. It took us a long time to find anyone. Many years after we started, we found someone. She [referencing Christine] always suspected but never really gave it much thought. That is, until another one came along. This young one [referencing Soraya] was very fascinated with us. Anytime she would visit, she would look at us and have a thousand mile stare. Instinctively she knew that there was something special, but being so young, did not know what it was. So, we had to wait. Wait for the time to be right and wait for her to develop a bit more.

Now after all of these years, here we are. We are standing tall and in our glory. We are working to help the world. We have not forgotten the past. Now that it is being written the right way, many will see what we have endured and what we have given.

Our names are very symbolic of the work that not only we are doing, but ALL of the towers are doing. We are transforming. We are going from a symbol of a time past to a beacon of light for the future. For some of us, it is from the run down and old to the new. People are waking up not only to the energy changes around them, but also to the thoughts and ideas of others.

While there is much that we could say about our past, there is so much more we can say about the future. We have been helping the other towers. Helping them in whatever way they may need us to. If it is to stand guard, we do so.

We will continue to be where we stand, physically helping guide ships, but energetically, we will be doing what is needed in the service of all.

Will we call out to others? Perhaps in time.

Will people know about us? Most definitely.

Will people look at us in a new light? Again, most definitely.

Teri, Ken's Twin Sister

Even though I was not physically born, I was energetically born. Not having a physical tower has, surprisingly, been a blessing. This is because I am able to travel to places that the others cannot and work with those that the others cannot. I have had to be quite patient while the others have been working, knowing that my turn to work and to shine would be coming. While I have been waiting, I have been working with my brother Ken. Yes, Ken is my twin, and since I do not have a tower, have been staying at his Tower. Together we work to support and help the other Towers. When we are not working, we bring an

This is the location where Teri's tower (Tower 10) was to be built.
While never built, she is here energetically.

atmosphere of fun. Our early history is not that interesting. Yes, you know that our Tower is near the point, and that it did provide a vantage out into the Harbor and the ocean. You already know what our purpose was, so no need to rehash that. Together with Florence and Ken, I was supposed to have been the third cog in the wheel. But sadly, they [referring to the builders] did not see fit to construct me. So, what to do since I was born, but had no home? I couldn't just float around in the ethers. No, I asked Ken if I could stay with him. He was and has been kind enough to let me do so. Together we are called Phoenix. It's a very apt name for us.

After he agreed to let me stay with him, we, like the others, waited out the war and waited for our fate. It was a good long while before someone came along and decided to put Ken's Tower to good use. They reconstructed a hell of a lot of it to be the control center for the ships. While I appreciate what they did, I do not appreciate that we were not honored formally. But, I digress. After it was reconstructed and things settled down, we started calling to people. There were many that, if they heard us, were not aware. And then there were others that heard the call but did not understand what it meant. And yet, there were only a handful more who heard the call and answered it. For some, we had to wait while they grew up. And for others, we had to wait for time to bring them back to us. And behold, we are working with two of them now. We call to people but in a very different way now. Now that we have been reawakened and are working on our destinies and legacies, we are calling to bring people to us who will make sure that our memories will carry on and that we will not be forgotten.

Even the restoration work that is occurring for some of us will be taken to a new level. It will be beyond what is currently being done now. We are beautiful and will continue to be for many, many more years.

Ken, Teri's Twin Brother

Our history is quite unique. The tower that you see today is not the tower that we started with. At the time of our birth, we were supposed to be two (2) towers. We were to be located closely together, so close that you could have thrown a ball and caught it. But, alas, in the time of war, everything changes. My sister's construction was planned for, but never seen to completion. Despite this, she is as strong as I am, and just as fierce, if you will. We are definitely equal and balance each other out.

As the years continued on, we became "forgotten." People would come and people would go never paying any attention to us. We called out, but seldom did anyone listen. We paused this briefly when the renovations were taking place. In many ways our renovations started to bring an awareness to people about our history and started tuning people into the idea of helping preserve us. Our renovations were significant – we were reduced in height and given a new physical purpose. We were to guide the ships. Because we have been renovated, we will stand for quite a while longer.

But enough about that. That is not the reason that you are reading this. You are reading this because you are curious to see things from our perspective and curious to know what we have to say. We have a lot to say, but we measure our words before saying them. We make sure that what we say is clear and that it can be understood. Our work, like the others, has taken us around the world. Often we work to help other towers, but at the same time, we do bring a sense of fun to what we do. Without it, it would be tedious. While it may seem like we have a small part to play in comparison to the others, we are happy to do it. Happy because we are also working on a task that is for the greater good and that is bigger than all of us. We have been working hard for many months, in your time, to help clean up and take care of this planet. There is so much that is unnecessary and so much that can be done to be better and make this a better place.

You [referencing humans] have given into your impulses and desires for far too long. You have forgotten the joy and value of helping others and not expecting anything in return. It is this that you need to come back to. It is this that will guide you and make you better. We are doing our part but need your help. There are some of you who are doing this. There are some of you who are already working hard to help us, and there are some that are waking up. Those that are working hard to help us are leveling up and raising not only themselves above others but also their [energetic] vibrations. They are creating a ripple effect that will help us touch many.

Yes, what we have done is help heal the park that we are in. But we have also expanded outward and healed the area around the park. I think you all call it Lewes. There is a very different energy there now than there was in the past. Because of the shift in energy, there will be more [people] who come and continue adding to the work that we do. They, too, will create a ripple and will touch others, outward and outward. Take what we have said to heart. You can be better than yourselves and let us be the reminder of that.

Florence

11

. . .

Florence (aka Tower 11) where her construction had been started, but was ultimately deconstructed.

I am Florence: I am one that is not seen but very readily felt. Like Teri, I was energetically born. I was to be built directly on the end of the point, but, like her, the humans thought that three there would be too many. I had started being constructed, but was taken down, and my materials were used for other structures. I do not have a physical tower, but am very much there energetically.

Since I am not physically there, I have the gift of being able to go many places that my fellow Towers cannot. I can go in the air, can go underground, can be on land or in the ocean. Of late, I have been working underground. There is also a history there and much that needs to be cleared. Just like there were civilizations that were lost to the ocean, there are those that were lost to the land. It is these that I am working with. I am also working with the spiritual centers of the world. Some of these you know because you can see them and others you do not because they are hidden. They are some of the hidden gems, overlooked and forgotten in many cases. They too are forming a network of energy and are often places where the lines [referencing ley lines] connect into. Their energy is something that can be felt at great distances and there is very much an aura around them. An aura that there is something mysterious but very special about them.

My work has kept me out and will keep me out longer. I have not returned "home" in a while, but that is ok. The work I do is of so much importance that I am ok not returning. Where my tower should have been is my home and that is where I go when I need a respite. On occasion I do help the others, but, since my task is quite complex, often I need as much time as I can to complete it.

There will be those who question whether what you read about me is true. I can tell you that there are no records of this in your human records, but those who are empathic and feel energy will feel me. They will get a very real sense of who I am and just how powerful I am and can be.

Frederick

...

Frederick (aka Tower 13) where he stands opposite
the entrance to the Cape May – Lewes Ferry Terminal in Cape
Henlopen State Park in Lewes, Delaware.

DELAWARE'S WATCHTOWERS

I am Frederick, one of the protectors of the Towers. As a protector, I work with the military and military installments. Trust me when I say that this takes a special touch. I work with them to ease the burdens that they carry so that those who remain here on Earth can take their rest and go home. I work directly with several archangels to do this. My work, like the others, is delicate, for the sacrifices those have made are beyond words. We have helped many and will continue to do so.

Like the other Towers, I have traveled around the world. You [referencing humans] are curious and would like to know where, but I cannot say. I cannot even tell Soraya who tracks our movements and plots our locations so that she can track the ley lines. Even though I cannot say, take comfort in knowing that all is going well.

My work has certainly not been easy, and because of it, I have had to ask for help. It has been freely given. I have used the help of the archangels, but also those of creatures, such as dragons. Each brings a special touch to the work that I do; ultimately making the work easier so that everything runs the way it is supposed to. As a watchtower, I am recognizable to many. Because I am so recognizable, I am approachable. Once approached, then my work begins.

My work has kept me away from home, but eventually I will get back there for some rest. My work, like the others is for something MUCH greater than ourselves. In some ways, it is comparable to the survival of a species. Where some fall, others rise. Where the old was, the new comes through. Change is always there and it is how you adapt to change that determines how strong you are. We are working with you and for you to make things better. Like you have heard my fellow Towers, we ask that you help us in return. Help others with no expectation of things in return. Love others and do not judge. Take care and treat things with respect. That is all we ask and will help lead to the betterment of all.

An Incredible Connection

• • •

Each Watchtower is beautifully unique in every way and, collectively, they are giving a gift to the world that will grow in magnitude as time passes. While it may seem unusual to connect and work with "inanimate" objects, such as the Watchtowers, I assure you that the relationship between us is very real; as real as someone receiving a visit from departed loved ones. To help give more context to the relationships that I have with all thirteen Watchtowers, I am lovingly sharing my story with how we connected and the work that I am doing with them.

Something Special

When one gazes upon the Watchtowers, there is much he can see. Does he see an old building and wonder what it was used for? Does he see the Tower as a home to its new residents, the birds and the vines? Or does he see something more? Does he look beyond the physical shell to see the beauty and complexity of the Watchtowers? As I reflect on my connection with them, I have come to realize that, in many ways, they have always been a part of who I am and are now helping me step into my task; a task that is not only greater than myself, but also one of tremendous value.

The Watchtowers called to me when I was a young child. As I visited Cape Henlopen State Park every summer, our communication was only that of sight, feeling, and wonder. As Phoenix stated, *"Early on, we were given the task of calling out to people. People who were gifted, who knew instinctively that there was more to us than the building that you see. It took us a long time to find anyone. Many years after we started, we found someone. She [referencing Christine] always suspected but never really gave it much thought. That is, until another one came along. This young one [referencing Soraya] was very fascinated with us. Anytime she would visit, she would look at us and have a thousand mile stare. Instinctively she knew that there was something special, but being so young, did not know what it was. So, we had to wait. Wait for the time to be right and wait for her to develop a bit more."*

As I grew up, developed, and stepped into my gifts of being an empathic clairvoyant, our relationship started to take on a new level of depth. One summer, when I was with a friend, we went to visit the Observation Tower (Tower 7). Everyone ran ahead to climb up, but yet, I paused. It was for the briefest of moments that I felt a tiny glimpse of what the Tower had seen and was feeling. From that moment on, that feeling stuck with me, and even to this day, I approach her Tower cautiously, always remembering on some level that first impression.

Not long after that visit, I took some "time off." Little did I know that during my sixteen years of "time off" there were other plans being made for me. During that time, the powers at be were lining up teachers and mentors, opportunities, and lessons. It took a reading with a psychic medium to start the beautiful chain reaction that led me back to the Towers and the work that we do today.

During my reading the topic of Reiki came up. The medium suggested that I look into taking some Reiki classes as a way to begin to understand my empathic gifts. I acknowledged the suggestion, but tabled the thought for a couple of years. One day out of the blue, while doing some serious housecleaning, I decided, on a whim, to take a Reiki class with a local Reiki Master. One Reiki class led to another Reiki class and to a second Reiki Master in Pennsylvania. On one of our breaks, I heard another student talking about an angel reading that she had with Christine Alexandria. While she could not remember where she had the reading, my classmate planted the seed. I thought about it the entire way home, and intrigued by this idea, I researched Christine Alexandria. I found that she did offer readings and signed up for one.

In my very first reading with Christine in 2017, Christine stated that I would be working with ley lines and would be mapping them. For a couple of days after my reading with her, I pondered it, but ultimately tabled the idea. However, the impression that Christine made stuck with me. Something felt very right when I was conversing with her; almost as if we were meant to meet. Because that feeling did not go away, I realized that I needed to learn more and try to figure out why it felt so right. As such, I signed up to be her student in the Angel Chatter Authorization Course, which is now called the BE You Program. After completing the course in 2018, I knew that I was to work with the Angelic realm.

With my desire to learn and my new validations of knowing my work was with the Angelic Realm, I signed up to be Christine's mentee, not once, but three times so far. It was during the second course of mentoring that not only the Watchtowers came forward, but also the subject of ley lines. My metaphysical work with the Watchtowers began during that time and has continued ever since. In the very beginning of working with the Watchtowers, we were learning about each other; me about who they were and what they experienced and them about me, my gifts, and how I can help them.

At first, it was to energetically clear three specific watchtowers. Then, as each one was cleared, to activate them to be energetic lighthouses that would help heal not only the area around them, but also help with the ley lines that they are on. As these original three watchtowers started their work, they activated the remaining towers and have helped them become energetic lighthouses.

Since that first introduction, both our work and my relationship with each tower has continued and evolved. I chat with them frequently; checking on how their work is going, whether they need help, and to ask questions of what is to come.

Our relationship grows more beautiful every day. It is an honor to not only work with but also learn from the Towers. It is also my honor to be able to tell their stories as they wish to share them. Our relationship has spanned a couple of decades so far and will continue for the remainder of my life. Our work will continue and will be shared as the Towers deem the time right.

As I continue to visit their physical Towers, I still gaze upon them with wonder, but also with a sense of knowing. A sense of knowing that, in some ways, we have come full circle and that I am where I am meant to be. I also have a sense of knowing perhaps what will come: that some will be lost to the ocean, that some will be honored with restorations, and others not. Regardless of how one sees them, they are truly something monumental to behold.

References and Photo Credits

• • •

Table on page 2

Grayson, W.C. (2005). *Delaware's Ghost Towers.* Authorhouse.

Map on Page 4

Fire Control Towers of the Delaware Coast. (2022, April 26). https://www.firecontroltowers.com/tower-locations.php

Photo credits

Cover & Tower Photos: All taken by Soraya Rose
Soraya's Photo: Taken by Sam Ellis of Sam Ellis Photography (https://www.samellis.com) and purchased by Soraya Rose

www.ingramcontent.com/pod-product-compliance
Lightning Source LLC
LaVergne TN
LVHW072023060526
838200LV00058B/4655